Dark and Light Verse

ALSO BY ALLEN IRELAND

Loners and Mothers

Dark and Light Verse

Poems by Allen Lee Ireland

David Robert Books

Published by David Robert Books
P.O. Box 541106
Cincinnati, OH 45254-1106

ISBN: 9781625493750

Poetry Editor: Kevin Walzer
Business Editor: Lori Jareo

Visit us on the web at www.davidrobertbooks.com.

Cover art: *Syria by the Sea*, Frederic Edwin Church

Acknowledgments

Grateful acknowledgment is given to the editors of the following journals, websites and newspapers in which 17 of the poems in this collection first appeared, some in slightly different form:

Blackfoot Valley Dispatch (Lincoln, MT): "Marysville"
The Boulder Monitor (Boulder, MT): "Elkhorn"
Button Eye Review: "Snow Walk"
The HyperTexts: "Warmth"
Lighten Up Online: "Recurring Tennis Dream," "Spring Break"
The Lyric: "Mountain Metropolis," "Small Step"
Pasque Petals (South Dakota State Poetry Society): "Heath"
Red Planet Magazine: "Holes"
Residential Collage (UNC-Greensboro): "Boy in Winter," "Ends Are Means"
The Road Not Taken: "Holy Book"
The Society of Classical Poets: "May Day," "Retired K-9"
Tiny Seed Literary Journal: "Nightmare"
WestWard Quarterly: "Property Marker"

Table of Contents

For all the carriers of light

VAN HELSING: There are darknesses in life, and there are lights; you are one of the lights.
MINA: But, doctor, you praise me too much, and—and you do not know me.

—Bram Stoker's *Dracula*

PART ONE: CHILDREN OF LIGHT

At the Public Library

I saw you in the children's stacks tonight:
A boy in glasses, with that look of light.
Each aisle was like a tunnel for your vision
Where choosing seemed a life-and-death decision.
At last you reached and pulled down for yourself
Heart of a Dolphin from the highest shelf.
You opened the slim, Mylar-covered prize
As light grew brighter in your dolphin eyes.
I stayed to watch: Would you reject or choose it?
You kept the book. . . . You will not keep the look.
Die young, my boy. Die young before you lose it.

Two Men in Love

Two men in love were standing on the edge
Of a cloudless cliff. "The world is beautiful,"
One said, "but also cruel. Suppose we just . . ."
"You can't be serious," the other said.
"I'm very serious," his lover said:
"We stand now at the apex of our love
In a world of hate. It couldn't get one whit better.
So on this day of perfect summer weather
Let's crown our love. . . ." And so they jumped together.
But when the hikers found them the next day
Their bodies were far apart, their faces pained
And bloody, turned coldly from each other. . . .
An old man, later, hearing of their fall,
Said simply, "Well, I guess it's best for all."

Hate Crime

It was not ice but hate
That knocked him off his feet.
He'd left the office late,
Walking on an icy sheet.

No: it wasn't ice
That made him slip and fall,
But the man who kicked him twice
For no reason at all.

Both his legs were broken.
His cries unheard
Grew faint, then were unspoken,
Like a lone baby bird's.

A mile away, later,
The night air held a chuckle:
"They'll think," thought the hater,
"The ice made him buckle!"

He froze there on the ground.
How terrible to die
Without a soul around
To know the reason why.

Boy in Winter

A wind like a car rushed by,
Sweeping the snow like dust,
And I watched through the frosty window
What would again be lost.

A spirit indifferent and free,
Intent on exploring the world,
Whirled through the woods and vanished,
And suddenly I was cold.

The streams were locked in ice.
The dens were sealed in snow.
But my soul was running, running
With the wind where I cannot go.

Couple Arguing

They remind me of other voices
That jarred me as a child,
Voices that clashed like cymbals
In an orchestra gone wild.

And added were the drumbeats
Of my heart inside my head. . . .
The neighbors fight all night.
I hear another war instead.

Chinese Box

Put bad memories in a box,
And lock it with a hundred locks,
Then stuff it deep in a trap-door safe
That not a soul, not even you,
Knows the combination to.
Then leave the room, and lock that, too.

The box, the safe, the room
Are in your mind of course.
And all those awful memories
Won't have to use a bit of force
To break each one of the iron locks
Protecting room and safe and box.
At any moment they're out again,
Unsummoned, not like genies. . . .

Bad memories are Houdinis.

A Fantasy

My life was a series
Of failures of fantasies—
Such towering trees
The dreamer would need
Skills bigger than trees
To scale and succeed.

The last climb concluded
With the crash of one deluded—
Of the fog about my head,
Of the unattainable tree,
Of the skills I never had,
Of the fantasy of me.

May Day

Such celebration is there round his grave!
The birds are singing, a cacophony
Of different keys. The wind is like a wave,
And all the flowers are tossing in its sea.
I hear the rattling drumbeat of a band.
Some kind of festival is going on.
Even the clouds are racing, yet I stand
As straight and still as cemetery stone.

My friend was once as full of life as this—
This razzle-dazzle with a clown on stilts,
And bagpipes played by men in saffron kilts,
And children splashing in the bright-blue lake. . . .
What feast of sight and sound! How sad it is
The dweller in the ground cannot partake.

Heath
(for Heath Ledger)*

I
Written in your genes
The day, hour and minute you would die.
Stealer of scenes.
Making those who did not know you cry.

You haunt the landscape like your namesake.
To ward you off, I sing a song:
"Skin too thin. Heart not strong.
It is amazing that you lived so long."

II
You could not sleep. You would not sleep.
But now your sleep is long and deep
Beside the sea-waves that so softly break. . . .
Are you amazed now that you cannot wake?

III
You were such a restless soul.
Will you leave your grave and wander
The way that Heathcliff did, the way
That you did from your nightly bed,
Haunting the streets of SoHo, playing homeless,
Your face as wasted as the dead?

IV
Your name evokes the rocks and vegetation
Of your home nation.

More like the rain-starved heath, though—
Its budding beauty
That can no longer grow.

*Heath Ledger was an Australian actor who died at the age of 28 of an accidental overdose of prescription medications. He was named after a diminutive of the character Heathcliff in *Wuthering Heights*.

Blood Moon

The scarlet moon is rising
Over Thompson's Ridge.
A boy runs home, dials 9-1-1,
And yells, "A fire is on the ridge!"

The operator calms him
As through the screen he sees
The full moon like a loosed balloon,
And feels the evening breeze.

Quenched and comforted by age
And the balmy scents of June,
The fire of youth dies down to sleep
Beneath the scarlet moon.

Mourning Paper

And here it is: your warm obituary.
But long before I saw it in these pages
Your seat had been reserved on Charon's ferry
And coldly recorded in The Book of Ages.

The boyish smile, the lightning in your eye:
That these went out at such an early age
Could not surprise. I didn't even cry . . .
All I did was sigh, and turn the page.

For the Children of Light*

It's true that you are doomed, defenseless,
And must not stray from who you are.
When the attacks are nasty, senseless,
Meant to injure or to jar,

Keep in mind you're a child of light
And you must turn the other cheek,
Being the darkest of the bright,
Being the strongest of the weak.

You're not a fighter: You're a hater
And can only attack when no one's there,
Screaming an hour later, a year later,
Into empty air.

*"When he walked out of the refuge of his study into the world and looked about him, he saw a place of torment, where creatures of prey perpetually thrust their claws into the quivering flesh of the doomed, defenseless children of light."—Theodora Bosanquet, *Henry James at Work*

PART TWO: A DOG'S LIFE

Retired K-9

When I was young, you kept me in a cage.
But as I got a little calmer, older,
Sometimes you'd let me ride up front with you
Shotgun, with my paw upon your shoulder.

It wasn't just for toys and treats, you know—
Sniffing out drugs and shells, and giving chase.
I gained a sense of honor/self-importance
And pleasure from the pleasure on your face.

My days are duller now, and you have found
Another K-9 friend to take my place.
For solace I have all your bathroom bottles
And, till the end, one evil cat to chase.

Sad Dog

Its nose and ears had been cut off.
At least it still could see.
And the sad expression in its eyes
Reminded me of me.

For some it's twisters flattening churches.
For others, cancer. But for me
A mutilated puppy proves
There is no deity.

Family Dog

All night he lies beside the sleeping children,
Their self-appointed sitter and protector,
Ready to bare his canines and to growl
At the approach of burglar or molester.

All day he sits before the outer door,
In case the children want to try the world—
So full of dangers for the curious boy,
So full of evils for the trusting girl.

He must protect them from the cars, the bullies,
The injurers of children everywhere.
And he must nip the hand of any parent
Reaching to lift them high or stroke their hair.

Flatlined

He knew his mistress was dying in her bed,
And because they were alone
He couldn't think of anything else to do
But knock the receiver off the phone
And call 9-1-1, which for a dog
Meant pressing with big paws the tiny keys
Randomly, frantically, and eventually
Making a panic sound like an EKG's.

Next day the girl who came to check on her
And to give the dog a dry meal and a bone,
Seeing him hangdog on her bare left leg,
At first formed an assessment very vague.
What made it register, what drove it home
Was the room-filling sound of the flat dial tone.

PART THREE: COLLEGE ASSIGNMENT

College

I went to sleep with certainty
Of far-succeeding days
When light would show again to me
The hills where I was raised.

It was as if some magic hand
Had moved me in the night,
For I awoke in a foreign land
Without a hill in sight.

It was as if they'd used me
To execute a plan,
For overnight, unwillingly,
I had become a man.

College Loner

A hummingbird just built his nest,
With a giant leaf for roof.
And now he perches like the rest,
Majestic and aloof.

It starts to rain: the other birds
Must tuck their heads beneath their wings.
The hummingbird is undeterred.
He straightens, and he sings.

And I, too, in my dorm,
The only place where I belong,
Am sheltering in the storm
Beneath my roof of song.

Holy Book

A book to him is like a woman who's
Above him, sacrosanct, mysterious—
A siren or a virgin or a queen
That he will never open, crack or touch.

He hears the title of a work of fiction
And goes all quiet. For it's often true
That men who cannot read the hallowed pages
Have more respect for them than those who do.

Reviews

One called it "anti-Nordic,"
Another, "anti-life,"
Another, "anti-Christian".
The book was like a knife,

But no less cutting than its critics.
Are there none to praise
The handle's classic craftsmanship
Or the gleaming beauty of the blade?

Nurse Ratched

Mildred Ratched, what a nurse!
As a matter of fact, she couldn't nurse worse.
Her touch is contagious, her prescription's a curse,
And all of her patients end up in a hearse.

Mildred Ratched, what a nurse.
When she tries to draw blood, it comes out in spurts.
The children scream, "It hurts! It hurts!"
And parents demand to see her certs.

Mildred Ratched, what a nurse.
Her manner's foreboding, her pleasure's perverse,
And no nurse in history has ever been worse. . . .
But what a wonderful subject for verse!

Verse

I used to be confined
Behind the bars of rhyme,
Tapping my feet to the steady beat
Of a second hand in my mind,
But always a little behind the time. . . .

And now I'm free! I'm free!
Even though
I do not know
What to feel, or dream, or be.

Recurring Tennis Dream

I want to play! I want to play!
But little things keep getting in the way.

My car won't start. My racket has a hole in it.
There's some new hindrance every other minute.

It takes a half an hour to tie my shoes.
(Maybe it's all because I think I'll lose???)

An indoor match, and yet I hear them say,
"There'll be a 90-minute rain delay. . . ."

The dream ends.
I never get to play.

Spring Break

Reading Nietzsche at 30,000 feet
In a window seat, pausing now and then
To look at clouds, or listen to the pilot
Speak over Zarathustra once again:

"Headwinds . . . tailwinds . . . turb over the Smokies. . . ."
Oh who could be happy or safe as I?—
In the hands of two all-seeing gods, homebound,
Reading Nietzsche, and flying high.

PART FOUR: MOTHER

Analogy

My mother's mother died when she was nine.
That same moment, somewhere across Earth,
A lion was killed just after giving birth.
The little girl and cub went on alone,
Struggled, grew up, had babies of their own.
But just as my mother found it difficult to be
Supporting and loving, so the lion's daughter
Looked at the strange things bawling and crawling on her
Unmoved, and with a kind of puzzlement,
Feeling no urge to nurture or protect.
And so she left her newborn cubs to die,
Wandering off into the wilderness . . .
Just as my mother (although she loved me dearly)
Was saying *I love you* a little insincerely.

White Widow

How did she regulate that sweet tooth she had?
She'd buy a block of chocolate and keep it in her purse,
Permitting herself just one square a day,
And offering me a square.
I would've eaten it all in one day!

And that other sweet she denied herself,
How did she manage to keep it so close
In the purse of her flesh
Without once opening
To share,
Or to scarf it down sneakily and guiltily alone?

O mother, O nun,
Who cleaned the house, drank coffee, and read magazines
While I amused myself in my room,
Were I and my brother the only joy
You received from the savory sweet?
Like the tree that doesn't feel the sugar in its veins,
Living darkly without pleasure
Only to bear fruit.

My Mother's Shadow

Messing with my mother's cat
While it was sitting in her lap,
I was astounded, taken aback

By the humanness that filled its eyes,
A look I really can't describe,
But which seemed to mock and mirror mine.

I came to this conclusion late:
Beings inarticulate
We often underestimate.

My mother sighs; the feline purrs. . . .
O thoughts for which there are no words!
O wisdom lost! Both its and hers.

Sentimental Attachment

We moved to the Smokies in '76—
A place my father called "the sticks,"
Where dinner was supper and creeks were cricks.

Our dog dug holes, so we named him Digger.
Each night we'd watch the moon get bigger
While being devoured by flea and chigger.

My mother, who liked it still as a mouse,
Was startled by hunters' shots at grouse.
All day she slaved in that old dark house. . . .

In 2020 she casually told
My brother and me, "The house is sold."
But I will buy it when I am old,

And dig her up (if I'm still able),
Plop her down at the kitchen table,
And finally win when we play Scrabble!

Warmth

The bird returned to incubate her egg.
But another bird had gotten to it first,
Giving the fragile shell a little poke
With his sharp beak, then sucking out the yolk,
Which rained down through the branches of the oak.
But still, the urge to nurture was so strong
She moved one leg, and then the other leg,
And sat down gently on the broken egg.

Like the mother who feels something is vaguely wrong
With her young son—some detriment unseen,
Some curled, dark abortion deep within—
And, even though she knows she cannot save,
Holds him through life, builds up, encourages . . .
Then warms the frozen grass beside his grave.

Memory Play

Something you told me stuck with me,
That in 1950,
In Santa Monica, California,
You saw *The Glass Menagerie* on a date.
And so I dreamed last night
That I was sitting on the other side of you
In that same domed theater,
Under a dripping dimming chandelier.
Even in darkness I could clearly see you:
The pretty profile of a girl of 17
Lit up from time to time by flashes from the screen.
Entranced,
You glanced
Only once at me, and very coldly,
With no interest,
With complete indifference,
As if you didn't know me!
I felt the way that unloved children feel
When they're rejected outright by their parents.
Of course we can't conceive
Our mothers had lives before we were conceived,
Or, if they did, those lives were meaningless.

I couldn't *believe*
You didn't acknowledge me.
As angry as Amanda in the penultimate scene,
I turned to you and yelled, "It's me! It's me!"
But you kept staring at *The Glass Menagerie*. . . .

Selfish dreamer!

A Call from Autumn Wind

"One of our staff left his keys in his car.
Your mother saw her opportunity
And sped off! But she only got as far
As Battle Branch. I guess she wanted to see
The house she'd lived in—was it 50 years?—
Before you moved her here. . . . The owner said
She stood before him on the verge of tears
And begged to sleep again in her old bed!
He brought her back to us, and now she's sleeping.
No charges of course. . . . Don't worry, we'll be keeping
A closer eye on her, and won't be leaving
Keys in our vehicles. . . . She's really very nice,
And funny, too! She said to us, near weeping,
What kind of son casts out his mother twice. . . .'"

PART FIVE: SCENES FROM BATTLE BRANCH

Property Marker

"What is this frippery we find
Along our walks through summer woods,
Rippling like water in the wind?
The woods are far too shady
For any flower at all.
Perhaps some wandering lady
Has let a ribbon fall
From her basketful of goods.
Or could some frolicking leaf
Have burned its candle at both ends,
And made an early Fall?"

"Come closer, child, and you will see
This patch of red could never feed
A single seed to bird or bee,
And only the poorest girl would wear
A faded ribbon in her hair.
It marks the southern boundary
Of someone's property."

"But no one lives here I can see."

"It's undeveloped land.
How can I make you understand?
Think of your hair, which is also red
And is the marker for your head,
Marking, like this, a thinking-spot,
Whether you use the space or not."

"No, Father, no, you are mistaken,
For can't you see the house forsaken,
By foliage almost overtaken,

Crumbling down to its foundation?
Even the little scrap of red
Is sinking in its mossy bed.
Nature owns this lot.
Nature owns *every* lot.
And She comes back,
Like vines on that firewood stack,
Like weeds through a sidewalk crack,
Whether we use the space or not."

Great Spirit

Although your omnipresence
Is world-renowned,
Your soul I never sense
On city ground.

Only among country trees
And freshest air,
In the midst of Nature's raucous peace
I feel you there.

Battle Cry

Today I heard the scream of a bird.
It sounded like the cry
Of an Indian chief with a crazed belief
That in battle he could not die.

This is the spot where the Cherokee fought
With arrow and knife and gun.
Their lives were lost. Their lands were lost.
And their spirits have dwindled to one.

And I could hear it! O feathered spirit
Whose war is never done,
Let loose your cry on this field of sky
And charge the whitest sun.

Victory on Fry Mountain

Dawn.
Like a bachelor Fry sleeps on
Under mounds of dirty linen,
And dreams of mountain women,
While far below, his love rises early,
Dresses in a hurry,
And scurries down the valley with her racket
And one ball. Aimlessly she whacks it
Against the wall, her hair a tangle, her bare feet
Sliding a little on the wet concrete.
She feels her ancestors
Watching—Cherokee warriors
Who fought the whites here and gave the land its name: Battle
  Branch.
Her vow to leave Fry's range
(*Today! Today!*)
Is stronger than her fathers' was to stay. . . .
The game begins. Her strokes
Are applauded by the windswept leaves of oaks.
She wins! The full sun
Is the gold championship plate of Wimbledon.
With head thrown back, arms raised,
She holds it, her wide eyes shining and dazed. . . .

Noon.
Fry's brow is stern,
Dark green with envy. His wash hangs dry
In a long still line across the sky.
Showing more muscle,
Mixing his strongest scents of pine and honeysuckle,
He waits. . . . The far-off clanking of a bell
Has broken the spell.

She stops, listens,
Remembering chores not done, mad chickens
Squawking for scratch. . . . Fry glows
Like a pleased god, accepting the sacrifice he knows
Is for him: a dead ball dropped,
A racket propped
By a torn net rippling in the breeze
On a cracked court covered with leaves.

Country Road

That old NO LITTERING sign
Threatening jail and a fine
Scares Man no more than the trees
That always unload
On the side of the road
Their autumn litter of leaves.

The slight humiliation
Of a deputy's citation
And the loss of a little cash
Does not prevent Man
From tossing a can
Of Coors, or McDonald's trash.

The littering tree
Pays a stiff penalty—
A season of freezing and death.
While the savage goes home
To his mate and his bone,
With the odor of beer on his breath.

In my dreams they escape,
Those chained inmates
On the roadside picking up,
And they bury the trash
That tossed this trash
Six feet deep at the dump. . . .

Dead Creek

It has no purpose now.
Its course is almost run.
It makes no sound, it feeds no deer,
And can't reflect the sun.

To move in darkness like a snail,
To live where no one comes. . . .
What is so wonderful about
Racing and gurgling in the sun?

Greetings

My giant window-tree
Has gashes and a serious break;
It offers me so many hands
I do not know which one to shake.

It bears no blossom, leaf or fruit:
It is a thawing tree,
Still reaching up to heaven,
And reaching out for me.

If trees at dawn can tap our windows,
Depressed with rain or dew,
Then can't you say, "*Good morning,*" friend,
When I say those words to you?

Snow Walk

It gives us now a little guiding-light,
Like a thick midnight forest's silver birches,
Or sculptured saints in empty darkened churches,
Or a black cavern's sparkling stalactite.
It gives each path an unextinguishable light,
Like even unspoiled sand on stormy shores,
Or a dark deserted mansion's marble floors,
Or a black cavern's gleaming stalagmite.

No rays pierce through tonight from moon or star;
No lamps illuminate our graveled lane;
The glow is out in hearth and window-pane;
And at this hour you'd never see a car.
The only light is from the settled snow.
In this dark world it's all the light we know.

Mountain Metropolis

The country is a city too, you know.
The wild geese sound a lot like honking horns.
The logging roads and trails are all dark alleys.
The summer homes invite you in like stores.

You scan the leaves like pages in a bookshop
On trees you'd find in any arboretum.
A hunter's shot could be an engine's backfire,
And every yard's a classic-car museum.

Eat blackberries at the meadow's breakfast bar,
Drink water from a fountain, rest on rock
No harder than a park-bench. Then look up:
The time is told you by that shimmering clock.

It's just like having London for a day
All to yourself, or Paris for a night.
Put down your cell: take in its blazing tower!
The stars come on at once like city lights.

PART SIX: THE INEVITABLE END

Elkhorn*

Only a few inhabit it today,
Unless you count the spirits peopling it—
The whores, the miners—and of course the elk
Circling it now the way they always did.

For social gatherings the townsmen built
Fraternity Hall in 1893.
Not one of all the dancers in the round
Envisioned silence for futurity.

Who builds a town on silver builds on sand.
Was there a corner in the namer's brain
That saw the horned and bright-eyed elk long past
The noise-filled Hall, the brothels, and the train?

*Elkhorn is an abandoned silver-mining town in western Montana.

Marysville*

I wonder if Tommy jinxed it when he named it
After a woman, for all it might forebode.
He should've named it Cruseville, for himself,
Who opened a vein, and found the mother lode.

"Just like a woman, ain't it?" the old men grouched.
Despite the gifts she gave, despite our labors,
Her heart dried up like Silver Creek in summer,
And now she is withholding all her favors.

*Marysville is a ghost town in western Montana, built and established around
the Drumlummon Mine in 1876 by founder Thomas Cruse.

Confederate Fountain*

For years the waters of dark history flowed
Beneath me, into me, and out of me.
I looked a little like a flooded lighthouse
Holding too long some remnant of the sea.

But it is over now: I lost my water
Before they craned me. (I bet I weighed a ton!)
I lost the placid looks of passersby.
I lost the birds. I lost the wind and sun.

I miss the constellations, the full climb
Of the cloud-colored moon, heavy and slow.
I miss the Rockies, huddled like old gossips,
White-haired, in their ragged shawls of snow.

But no one cares. Not even the ones who shouted
At city and at sky to leave me be.
They care for country, causes, legacies.
The people's hearts are stone for stone like me.

*The Confederate Memorial Fountain was removed from Hill Park in Helena,
Montana, in August, 2017.

Plague

You'd think it was some kind
Of a disease—
Hair falling out,
Skin blotched,
Back bent.
They say all these
Are symptoms of the end.

You'd think it was
Contagious—
You who daily watch it
Grow worse and worse,
Afraid to come too close,
Afraid
You might catch it.

Good God!
You'd think it was a curse!

Nightmare

A little flickering fire upon a hill
We've had our eye on for a while, until
It suddenly decides to be our fate,
Jumping the road with no fuel but its will,
Expanding to be sure that it engulfs us,
The way a snowball grows the more you roll it.
Can you not sense how personal it is?
It's just for you, and you feel privileged,
For no one ever loved you more than this.
The fire does not incinerate you, though:
It sweeps you up into a safer space,
A heavenly zone above the hellish flames.
For nothing can kill us in our nightly dreams.
We go on as a soul . . . then wake with screams.

Dead Sleep

Even from my deepest dream-filled sleep
Sometimes I am awakened by a sound—
My phone's vibration, or a car alarm,
Or lightning, or a siren through the town.

Dear Science, I must have your reassurance:
Please tell me for my soul's (and pity's) sake
It's possible to sleep, to sleep for eons,
And never once awake.

Birthdays

A birthday is an awful thing:
The less-than-perfect gift,
The multitude of candles
That prove you haven't lived.

They tell you that you're older;
You're older than they know.
And every wish you ever made
Is burning as you blow.

So blow again, until you spend
Your last and deepest breath!
Burnt wax and wick will make you sick
Like the waft of death.

Killer's Note

"Done because we are too menny,"
Wrote Father Time to Jude.
So Mother Nature writes us
In language just as crude

And letters so colossal
An idiot could read
Through distance or the dormant fog
Of a religious creed.

"Done because we are too menny,"
She plainly says.
"My sereal merderers and kansers
And wores and plaigs."

*In Thomas Hardy's novel *Jude the Obscure*, Little Father Time kills his two half-siblings and then hangs himself.

To Spring

They took away her capital letter!
And now she is no loftier or better
Than a little water snaking from the ground,
Or any other coil you can't keep down. . . .

It fits the age, though, what they've done to spring:
No reverence anymore for anything.

Death Chamber

Before the doctor injected him
He remembered how as a kid
His mother and father had always protected him
No matter what he did.

Behind the cracked and dirty plexiglass
He knew they would be there:
His father, trembling, determined not to cry,
His tortured mother, mouthing a silent prayer.

The poison's in. He looks to them
But cannot find them in the faceless crowd.
They waited 20 years to watch him die. . . .
And now their heads are bowed.

Symbol

It flies a little, and then it falls.
It does not flap
Its fine wings when the warden captures it,
And in his car sits docile on his lap

All the way to the rehabber,
Who welcomes with bright eyes this precious find,
And tells him, when he asks what is the matter,
The broad-winged hawk is blind.

The warden's eyes go dark.
He thinks, *What is the point of such a life?*
We might as well just end it
With a bullet or a knife.

Farsighted

His distant, searching eyes alighted
On someplace out of sight and sound.
But, instead of the astronomer excited
By what his scope has found,
He looked like the farmer who foresees a bad harvest,
Then dropped his gaze, and frowned:
Eyes that see the farthest
Are fixed upon the ground.

The Woman in the Water

As the bathtub slowly fills,
She opens a bottle of sleeping pills.

The mirror reflects, as she prepares for death,
The face of a woman excited, holding her breath.

Grandly she steps in, as though it were a yacht or mansion's
   pool. . . .
The bottle is empty, and the bathtub is full.

She has dreamed that what will soon occur
Will be the happiest thing that ever happened to her.

But suddenly to her surprise
A few tears trickle from her eyes.

Ends Are Means

It was as if a storm raged through
The quiet quarters that we knew—
A menace of such magnitude
We could not help but call it good.
For after rain and wind were done
Horizons cleared, and kept us one.

Some call it death, some call it doom
That wreaks such havoc in the home,
That tries to rip from solid sod
What's built of brick and blessed by God.
But we have learned from every blast
Without the storm we would not last.

A Question

You're depressed because nothing lasts.
What is the point, you ask,
Of getting out of bed in the morning?
Of trying to build something?

You're right.
You're absolutely right.
Not even the universe is eternal.

But isn't it close enough?

PART SEVEN: FOUND IN SPACE

Small Step

Did you travel here for fame,
To immortalize your name,
To stake your country's claim?
Or was there, deep inside, another aim?

Did you think this other world
Toward which your craft was hurled,
For which our flag was left unfurled,
Would bring you closer to your little girl?*

Separated from your race,
Did you finally feel the grace?
Did you see your daughter's face
In the silence and the space?

*Neil Armstrong's daughter died of leukemia at the age of two.

Stargazing

A walking, not a sitting light,
And not a shooting star,
Twinkling, but not bright,
Distant, but not far,
Delicate, shy, determined light . . .
A plane at night.

Man of Jello

Look, it's a bird. Look, it's a plane. . . .
No, wait. It's just that flying dude
Who's in love with Lois Lane.
Love is stronger than Superman!
(It's really Love that is his kryptonite.)
Sure, he can stop a meteorite,
Can turn Lex Luthor's "land"
Into a satellite.
But Love can do what he can't do:
Love can set the whole world right!

A COVID Christmas (2020)

Saturn has a mask of rings,
Like Jupiter's, homespun.
The two are social distancing
As they meet around the sun.

Meanwhile, infected Earth
Is quarantined below.
For mandates do not work,
And vaccines are slow.

Jupiter and Saturn
Have formed a Christmas star!
But this time it's the wise men
Who are staying where they are.

Sirius and the Lawman

The night star said to the sheriff,
"It's only a star by your lapel:
One out of many, just like me.
No one would care if it fell."

"Even so," said the sheriff,
"I'll keep it shined as bright as you,
And the people will look up to me,
And wish for justice swift and true."

Said the night star, "I can't grant
The wishes wished on me."
Said the sheriff, "Nor can I. . . .
But we are reverenced equally.

And whether it's God or the Devil
That fells this badge of steel,
It will leave a hole forever
That everyone will feel!"

Just then the storm-clouds gathered,
Darkening all the skies,
And the only stars still shining
Were in the sheriff's eyes.

A Sunray Lands in Syria

Forged in the sun's furnace
And shooting through its surface
Like an anvil's spark,
Like sperm from a penis,
I make my headlong journey through the dark,
Past Mercury's egg, past Venus,
And hope to bring to birth
Something beautiful on Earth.

Oh I could green a blade of grass,
Refract the patterns in St. Peter's glass,
Add one freckle
To a Turk's-cap petal,
Or sheen to an Olympic silver medal. . . .
But the happiest of us die
Giving light to a woman's eye.

Instead I come to trouble.
Like the Syrian rebel,
Once a boy
Who played street hockey here with a rebellious joy,
My light goes out beneath a pile of rubble.

Holes

A star dies. The universe
Buries it in a black hole,
With no marker for its body
Or service for its soul.

The galaxy wears black
(But then it always does).
The preacher God is silent
(But then He always was).

The death of UY Scuti,
Or Earth, or human race:
It is all one, you see,
In the potter's field of space.

I Must Thank . . .

1) Tyler Knott Gregson, whose debut book of poems sold 120,000 copies and who has over 300,000 followers on Instagram, numbers I could only dream of. I expected him to throw me a meatless bone, but instead he gave me great joy, reassurance, and confidence.

2) Fred Chappell, whose blunt, microscopic critique of my poems always makes them better. It still amazes me that he takes time away from his glistening writing to wade with me through the darkness.

3) My mother. No need to elaborate.

4) Kevin Walzer and Lori Jareo of WordTech, for their willingness to take me on a second time, despite this book's controversial elements. Without them my poems would have been handed down on loose leaves of paper to a few surviving relatives, and lost forever.

About the Author

Allen Ireland lives in Helena, Montana, and works for law enforcement administration. His childhood home on Battle Branch in Bryson City, North Carolina, has been sold, but his memory and imagination still putter there daily. Mr. Ireland welcomes feedback from readers and can be reached at allenireland69@hotmail.com.

Made in the USA
Monee, IL
18 April 2021